Date Due

Convertibles

Thomas Streissguth

Capstone Press

MINNEAPOLIS

Printed in the United States of America.

Capstone Press • 2440 Fernbrook Lane • Minneapolis, MN 55447

Editorial Director   John Coughlan
Managing Editor   John Martin
Production Editor   James Stapleton

Library of Congress Cataloging-in-Publication Data

Streissguth, Thomas, 1958-
 Convertibles / by Thomas Streissguth
  p. cm. -- (Cruisin')
 Includes bibliographical references and index.
 ISBN 1-56065-256-X
 1. Automobiles, Convertible--Juvenile literature.
[1. Automobiles, Convertible.] I. Title. II. Series
TL147.S77 1996
629.222--dc20   95-7115
                                              CIP
                                               AC

Table of Contents

Chapter 1

With the Top Down

You reach for the latch on the top of the windshield. Your hand moves to a switch on the dashboard. An electric motor gently pulls back the top. In seconds, your car is open to the sky.

There's nothing like cruising in a convertible. You can see more of the passing scenery. The sun warms your face, and a breeze blows through your hair. You're not just driving. You're having fun.

Car makers once nearly stopped making convertibles. Today, however, convertibles are more popular than ever. Nearly all North American and foreign car companies make at least one open car. And older convertibles in good condition have become valuable collector's items.

Chapter 2

Convertible History

Open cars have been around for a long time. In fact, all the earliest cars were open. In these "horseless carriages," a motor replaced the horse as the power source. Early cars still looked like horse carriages. Some manufacturers sold a **canvas** top as an extra **option**.

Open Cars and Closed Cars

Later, new versions of this motorized carriage appeared. People called them roadsters, runabouts, or touring cars. Ford made its first Model A roadster in 1903. The

This Indy 500 pace car, one of the world's best-known convertibles, circles the track just before the big race.

Model A came with either a leather or rubber top.

During the 1920s, auto makers sold many more closed cars than open cars. But the car with the removable top survived. In 1928, manufacturers began calling these cars "convertibles."

For the next 11 years, car makers designed all their convertible tops to open **manually.** Drivers raised and lowered their tops by hand. In 1939, Plymouth built the first automatic top, raised and lowered by vacuum power.

In 1940, Ford offered the first electric motors for convertible tops. The 1941 Oldsmobiles came with hydraulic pumps that worked even better than vacuum power.

Home from the War

In 1945, World War II ended. Millions of soldiers returned home from the fighting. Driving down the highway in an open car was an important part of their dreams of a new life.

Car makers were ready for these customers. They cut off the tops of their standard models. They replaced the steel roofs with canvas tops. A sheet of plastic replaced the rear window. Many soldiers bought these inexpensive convertibles.

The Porsche 911 will take you down the road as fast as any convertible on the market.

The Golden Age of the Convertible

The convertible became more and more popular. For many people, it symbolized youth and freedom. Most car companies had at least one convertible model.

One of the favorites was the two-seat Thunderbird convertible. Ford made the car from 1955 until 1957. It had an optional

fiberglass hardtop that drivers could snap into place.

During the 1950s, car makers made larger and fancier convertibles. They switched to electric motors for raising and lowering the tops.

In 1957, the Ford Motor Company introduced the Skyliner. This was a convertible with a steel top instead of the usual canvas top.

This 1938 Oldsmobile, with whitewall tires and a rear "jump seat," brings its owners to the picnic in style.

The Skyliner had a complex system of electric motors to slide the two-part steel top into the trunk. The Skyliner was heavy and expensive. Its switches and motors often broke down. Ford sold the car for only three years.

Mustangs

The 1960s were the heyday of the convertible. Ford introduced the convertible Mustang in 1965. Although the Mustang looked and performed like a sports car, it was not an expensive car.

It had bucket seats and a three-speed stick shift on the floor. Buyers could choose from a wide range of options. Instead of the standard six-**cylinder**, 101-**horsepower** engine, owners could buy a more powerful **V-8 engine**. They could also choose a four-speed transmission.

The Mustang was one of the nation's most popular cars. The year it appeared, 1965, was the biggest year ever for convertibles. More than 500,000 **ragtops** rolled off the assembly line in 1965.

Ford brought back the Mustang convertible in the 1980s.

But big changes were coming. New freeways made it possible to drive at higher speeds. But driving at high speed in a convertible was like driving in a wind tunnel.

Many people wanted practical family cars, too. Convertibles were not practical. They were hard to heat, and they leaked in rainy weather. Their tops rattled, and their plastic back windows turned cloudy. And thieves could easily cut through a canvas top.

Safety Problems

During the 1970s, convertibles faced a new problem. Some studies showed that convertibles were unsafe. An accident, the studies said, could throw passengers out of the car. Convertibles were especially dangerous in

Two-seat roadsters, such as this German Porsche, have become classic collector's items.

Driving with the top down is a fun way to spend a sunny day.

a rollover accident. A steel roof would provide much more protection than a canvas top—especially a lowered canvas top.

Ford stopped making convertibles in 1967. American Motors Corporation made its last convertible in 1968. Chrysler produced no more after 1971.

On April 21, 1976, a white Cadillac El Dorado convertible rolled off the General

Motors assembly line. Almost 20 feet (6.1 meters) long, this car had a 500-cubic-inch V-8 engine. It weighed 5,000 pounds (2,268 kilograms). The car had power windows, power steering, and power locks. The interior was white leather.

The Dodge Viper is a high-performance machine with quick acceleration, good handling, and a sporty look.

It was a beautiful car. But GM would make no more. Many people believed that the 1976 El Dorado was the last convertible.

Chapter 3

The Convertible Returns

In the late 1970s and early 1980s, many people were still buying and driving new convertibles. But these convertibles were made in Europe, where car companies were still making open-top sports cars. The British made the MG and Triumph Spitfire convertibles. Italian car makers were producing the Fiat 124 and Alfa Romeo Spider convertibles.

These cars were popular in North America. As open cars became rare, drivers began to miss them. They forgot the problems of owning a convertible. A wave of **nostalgia** for the convertible began.

Convertible Conversions

To meet the demand for new convertibles, there were a few firms that offered a special service to turn closed cars into convertibles. One of these **conversion** companies was Emess Coach Builders of Clearwater, Florida.

At Emess, customers brought in their closed sedans. The mechanics would go to work. They sliced off the roof. Then they **reinforced** the frame of the car with new steel supports.

It was important to reinforce the car's frame. Removing the top weakened the frame. Without a solid roof, the body sagged and eventually collapsed. But a reinforced frame made a converted car heavier and more expensive than a closed car.

Emess workers also installed a new windshield with clamps to hold down the top. Then they put the new top in place. Most of the new tops were automatic. A switch in the dashboard controlled a small electric motor run by the car's battery. The motor powered a pair of **hydraulic cylinders** that pushed the top up to close and pulled it back to open.

The Return of the Ragtop

In the early 1980s, Chrysler and other makers could see that many people missed convertibles and that the conversion companies were doing a good business. In 1982, Chrysler put a new convertible on the market. They made the Dodge Reliant K-Car into a convertible known as the LeBaron.

Ford and GM followed Chrysler's lead. Ford offered a new convertible GTL Mustang. GM built Chevrolet Cavalier, Buick Riviera, and Pontiac 2000 Sunbird convertibles. The convertible was back.

Chapter 4

Imported Convertibles

Car makers in Europe never stopped making convertibles. Open sports cars have always been popular there. Ferrari, Porsche, Alfa Romeo, and many other companies still make and sell them. And other companies are coming out with new versions and offering them in the big North American car market.

The Triumph TR-8 is one of the most famous of the British roadsters.

Here are some of the hottest imported convertibles.

Alfa Romeo Spider

Alfa Romeo, an Italian company, made the Spider roadster from 1966 to 1994. There are two versions of this open car—the Spider and the Spider Veloce. Both have an inline, four-cylinder engine that gets 120 horsepower. In both cars, the shifter sits on the center console, instead of on the floor. The tops of both are opened manually.

The Spider Veloce has alloy wheels, soft leather seats, larger tires, and a removable hardtop.

Audi Cabriolet

In 1994, Audi, the German company, produced its first convertible, the Audi **Cabriolet**. The Cabriolet's top is automatic. Drivers turn a simple T-shaped handle to release the top. A quiet electric motor lowers the windows and folds back the cloth top. The

A removable hardtop came with the Spider Veloce, which Alfa Romeo stopped making in 1994.

motor also operates the rear **boot**, which covers the top when it is down.

The Cabriolet is a strong and steady car. Heavy reinforcement in the doors and frames gives it a solid feel in high wind and on rough roads, even with the top down.

The beautiful Jaguar XJ-S.

Bentley Continental

The Bentley Continental is expensive. Its **base price** runs about $270,000. The Continental is actually a Rolls-Royce Corniche without the Flying Lady, the Rolls Royce hood ornament.

This car has a massive, 6.75-liter V-8 engine. The interior features rugs of lamb's wool, wood trim, and deep leather seats. The top is fully automatic.

Ferrari 348 Spider

The Spider is a road car that feels like a race car. A powerful 310-horsepower V-8 engine can make 60 miles (97 kilometers) per hour in 5.7 seconds. Drivers raise and lower the top manually. A one-piece leather boot covers the lowered top.

Jaguar XJ-S

Many people think that the British Jaguar company makes the best cars in the world. They also think that the XJ-S convertible is the best modern Jaguar on the road.

There are two versions of this luxury car. One has a 4.0-liter, inline six-cylinder engine that delivers 237 horsepower. The other has a mighty 6.0-liter, V-12 engine that gets 301 horsepower. Computer systems control both, and both offer electronic, four-speed transmissions.

The XJ-S interior has walnut wood trim. Its seats, dashboard, and steering wheel are leather. The top is thickly padded and fully automatic.

Ferrari Mondial

This Ferrari is a four-seater with a manual top. The 3.4-liter V-8 engine gets 300 horsepower with excellent handling and braking. The Ferrari is an instant collector's item.

The Mazda Miata, one of the least expensive imported convertibles, is popular among younger drivers.

Ferrari, an Italian company, makes some of the world's best-known sports cars.

Mazda MX-5 Miata

The Japanese Miata is a best-seller in North America. One of the least expensive imported cars, it looks like a classic European roadster. Under the hood is a 1.8-liter, 128-horsepower, four-cylinder engine. The top is sturdy and weatherproof.

Chapter 5

Some American Convertibles

American convertibles made a strong comeback in the 1980s and 1990s. Today, open cars make up about 3 percent of the total new car market. The Chrysler LeBaron, the first modern convertible, remains the most popular.

GM, Ford, and Chrysler are trying to make their new models practical as well as fun. They have made the convertible safer by adding airbags and seat belts. The new open cars are also sturdier and more comfortable. Their roofs leak less, and in high winds the cars hold the road better than older models.

Here are some of the current stars of the American convertible market.

Chevrolet Camaro

For a few years during the 1980s, GM hired conversion firms to make convertibles from its hardtop models. The Camaro Z28, the first convertible the company made, was first produced in 1969.

The Camaro's automatic roof lowers into a three-piece, plastic boot. The rear window is glass, not plastic. The Z28 offers good protection against water damage, a common problem in convertibles.

The **overhead-valve** V-8 engine delivers 275 horsepower. The Camaro drives like a high-performance sports car.

Chevrolet Corvette

GM has built a million Corvettes since the 1950s. It is the most popular sports car made in North America. Many drivers will not buy any other car.

The 300-horsepower V-8 engine makes the Corvette one of the fastest convertibles on the road. Chevrolet has improved the car's suspension and changed the seats and front console. A heater keeps the glass rear window clear. The top operates manually.

The car's designers have thought of everything, even the stereo system. When the

Corvettes have always had a low, sleek look that makes them easy to spot on the highway.

driver lowers the top, the car's speakers automatically raise their volume.

Ford Mustang GT

The GT descends from the classic 1965 Mustang. A new, smoother shape makes the GT more **aerodynamic**. It is a two-door, four-passenger car that comes with either a V-6 or a V-8 engine.

The power top is one of the quickest on the market, folding back in about 15 seconds. A

The Dodge Viper RT/10

Chrysler brought back the convertible with the LeBaron, an open version of the Dodge Reliant K Car.

vinyl boot covers the top, which hides in a space behind the rear seat. With no top stacked over the back seat, the driver can see better behind the car.

The V-10 engine of the Dodge Viper gets this car up to freeway speed faster than a Ferrari.

Dodge Viper

A high-performance roadster, the Viper has a powerful 8.0-liter, V-10 engine. It **accelerates** from 0 to 60 miles (0 to 97 kilometers) per hour in just 4.5 seconds. This is even faster than the Ferrari Spider.

The Viper's manual top folds between the windshield and a fixed platform over the back seat. The windows snap on and off, and the driver can also remove the rear window.

Pontiac Firebird

The Firebird comes in a V-6 and a V-8 version. The car's designers took special care to build a solid, watertight top. And they built

Corvettes look as good in motion as they do standing still. Some collectors wouldn't buy any other car.

Convertibles have made a strong comeback after nearly disappearing from the roads in the late 1970s. With more models hitting the market in the 1990s, drivers now have a wide choice of styles, sizes, and speeds.

the body low to the ground, so the car keeps steady in strong winds. The Firebird also boasts one of the best sound systems of any convertible.

Glossary

accelerate–to increase speed

aerodynamic–shaped to move smoothly and easily through the wind

base price–the price of the basic vehicle without any additional equipment

boot–a cover for a lowered convertible top

cabriolet–a French word Europeans use for convertibles

canvas–a sturdy fabric car makers used to make early convertible tops

conversion–the changing of one body style to another

cylinder–the can-shaped chamber of an engine where the fuel burns

fiberglass–plastic-like material made of small glass fibers

horsepower–a measure of engine strength

hydraulic cylinders–fluid-filled chambers that transfer energy to raise and lower convertible tops

manual–operated by hand

nostalgia–a fondness for the past

option–an extra part or feature that buyers can order for their cars

overhead-valve engine—an engine with valves mounted on top of the cylinders

ragtops–a slang term for convertible cars

reinforce–to strengthen by adding new parts

V-8 engine–an engine with eight cylinders arranged in a "V" formation

valve–opening through which gasoline and air enter an engine's cylinder

To Learn More

Gunnell, John. *Convertibles: The Complete Story*. Blue Ridge Summit, Pennsylvania: Tab Books, 1984.

Hirsch, Jay, and Warren Weith. *The Last American Convertibles*. New York: Collier Books, 1979.

Photo Credits

Petersen Publishing: pgs. 4, 6-7, 8, 10, 11, 12, 15, 16, 17, 20, 24-25, 26, 29, 30, 31, 32, 37, 38, 39, 40, 41, 42

Chrysler Corporation: pgs. 18-19, 34

Some Useful Addresses

Magazines

Hot Rod
6420 Wilshire Boulevard
Los Angeles, CA 90048-5515

Motor Trend
6420 Wilshire Boulevard
Los Angeles, CA 90048-5515

Road & Track
1499 Monrovia Avenue
Newport Beach, CA 92663-2752

World on Wheels
1200 Markham Road
Scarborough   ONT M1H 3C3
Canada

Index